PROBLEM SOLVED!

YOUR TURN TO THINK BIG

Innovations in Everyday Technologies

Larry Verstraete

 Crabtree Publishing Company

www.crabtreebooks.com

Crabtree Publishing Company
www.crabtreebooks.com

Author: Larry Verstraete

Series research and development: Reagan Miller

Editorial director: Kathy Middleton

Editors: Crystal Sikkens, Janine Deschenes

Proofreader: Petrice Custance

Designer: Ken Wright

Cover design: Ken Wright

Photo researchers: Ken Wright, Crystal Sikkens

**Production coordinator
and prepress technician:** Ken Wright

Print coordinator: Katherine Berti

Cover: (background) The innovation of the pop-top can; (top left) The innovation of the toothpaste tube; (top right) The invention of the vacuum cleaner; (bottom right) The invention of the pop-up toaster

Title page: Making a pincushion to wear on the wrist was an innovation that made pins handier for sewers.

Photographs

Alamy: Photo Researchers, Inc, p 4 (left); Granger Historical Picture Archive, p 4 (right)

AP Images: Robert F. Bukaty, p 21 (bottom)

Getty Images: Bruce Kluckhohn p 11; Bettmann, p 15; Hulton Archive, p 16; Science & Society Picture Library, p 18–19 (bkgd), p 24 (top right);

Granger: Granger, NYC, p 9 (top right)

iStock: © elgol, p 7 (bottom); © EyeJoy, p 14 (bottom)

Shutterstock: Gil C, p 17 (top right);

Wikimedia: title page; p 6; p 8 (bkgd); United States public domain, p12; p 13; p 18 (left); Blake Burkhart, p 20 (bkgd); p 20 (top right); p22–23 (bkgd); Yuya Sekiguchi, p 22; United States public domain, p 25 (top right)

All other images by Shutterstock

Library and Archives Canada Cataloguing in Publication

Verstraete, Larry, author
     Innovations in everyday technologies / Larry Verstraete.

(Problem solved! your turn to think big)
Includes index.
Issued in print and electronic formats.
ISBN 978-0-7787-2678-4 (hardback).--
ISBN 978-0-7787-2684-5 (paperback).--
ISBN 978-1-4271-1805-9 (html)

     1. Technology--Juvenile literature. 2. Technological innovations--Juvenile literature. 3. Inventions--Juvenile literature.
I. Title.

T48.V46 2016   j600   C2016-904155-7
                                            C2016-904156-5

Library of Congress Cataloging-in-Publication Data

Names: Verstraete, Larry, author.
Title: Innovations in everyday technologies / Larry Verstraete.
Description: New York, NY : Crabtree Publishing Company, [2017] |
     Series: Problem solved! Your turn to think big | Includes index.
Identifiers: LCCN 2016026661 (print) | LCCN 2016030056 (ebook) |
     ISBN 9780778726784 (reinforced library binding) |
     ISBN 9780778726845 (pbk.) |
     ISBN 9781427118059 (Electronic HTML)
Subjects: LCSH: Technology--Juvenile literature.
Classification: LCC T48 .V47 2017 (print) | LCC T48 (ebook) |
     DDC 600--dc23
LC record available at https://lccn.loc.gov/2016026661

Crabtree Publishing Company
www.crabtreebooks.com   1-800-387-7650

Printed in Canada/102016/IH20160811

Published in Canada
Crabtree Publishing
616 Welland Ave.
St. Catharines, Ontario
L2M 5V6

Published in the United States
Crabtree Publishing
PMB 59051
350 Fifth Avenue, 59th Floor
New York, New York 10118

Published in the United Kingdom
Crabtree Publishing
Maritime House
Basin Road North, Hove
BN41 1WR

Published in Australia
Crabtree Publishing
3 Charles Street
Coburg North
VIC, 3058

CONTENTS

Washing Dishes

When your kitchen becomes cluttered with dirty dishes, you might do what millions of others do—load up the dishwasher, turn a dial or press a button, and sit back while the machine does the work. Over 100 years ago, there were no dishwashers to make life easier. It wasn't until Josephine Cochran became so frustrated with finding chipped hand-washed dishes that she decided to invent a machine to wash them instead.

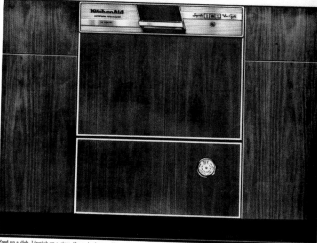

Josephine Cochran created a company called Garis-Cochran Manufacturing Company to build her dishwashers. Her company later became part of KitchenAid®.

In 1949, KitchenAid® introduced the first dishwasher to the public, which was based on Josephine Cochran's design.

Inventions and Innovations

An invention is a product or process that is the first creation of its kind. Josephine Cochran's original dishwasher is an invention. An innovation is a change or improvement to an existing invention. The dishwasher now used in many homes is an innovation because it has modern features that improved upon Josephine Cochran's invention.

Inventors and **innovators** solve a problem or meet a need. They have made life easier and more enjoyable for us with everyday products, gadgets, and materials. Perhaps the stories in this book will inspire you to be a problem-solver, too. The next great invention could be yours!

Thanks to Josephine Cochran's invention, many people now have dishwashers in their homes.

Zapped!

Today, more kitchens have microwave ovens than dishwashers. We place cold food inside a microwave, press a few buttons, and then enjoy hot and steamy food a few minutes later. For this amazing time saver, we have to thank its inventor, British **engineer** Percy L. Spencer.

Engineers use science and math to solve problems or meet needs. Sometimes, engineers can also be inventors and innovators, when they make new solutions or improve on existing ones. Inventors, innovators, and engineers all share the same **traits**, such as curiosity and creativity.

The first microwave ovens were called radar ranges. They were about the size of a refrigerator and very expensive.

How did it happen?

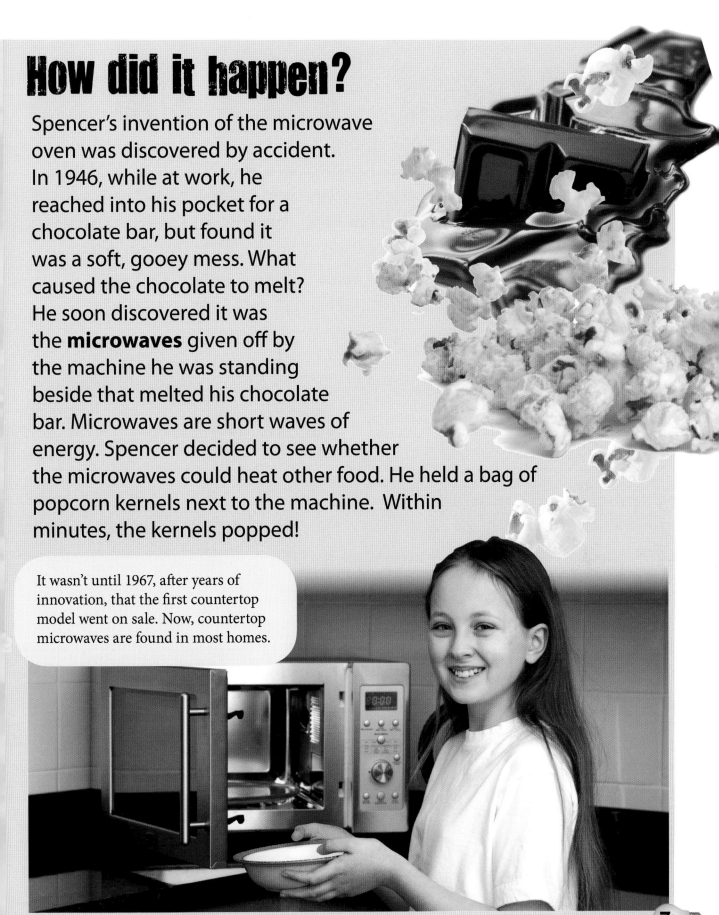

Spencer's invention of the microwave oven was discovered by accident. In 1946, while at work, he reached into his pocket for a chocolate bar, but found it was a soft, gooey mess. What caused the chocolate to melt? He soon discovered it was the **microwaves** given off by the machine he was standing beside that melted his chocolate bar. Microwaves are short waves of energy. Spencer decided to see whether the microwaves could heat other food. He held a bag of popcorn kernels next to the machine. Within minutes, the kernels popped!

It wasn't until 1967, after years of innovation, that the first countertop model went on sale. Now, countertop microwaves are found in most homes.

Perfect Every Time!

Electric toasters of today look nothing like the ones 100 years ago. The earliest electric toasters only heated bread one side at a time. They also didn't have heat controls, so the toast often burned. Charles Strite changed that. In 1919, Strite ordered toast in the cafeteria at his work. When a hard, black slice arrived on his plate, Strite decided it was time to change the electric toaster.

Early electric toasters, such as this one from 1910, often burnt the toast. They were also dangerous to use.

Pop-up

In his home workshop, Strite created a model that toasted bread on both sides. It had a timing device and springs to make sure the toast popped up crisp and golden brown. By 1930, after some innovation, a **thermostat** was added to control the temperature. This was a perfect way to avoid burnt toast!

There were many advertisements during the 1930s that promoted the new pop-up toaster.

Today, most toasters use springs, thermostats, and timers to make sure our toast pops up just the way we like it.

Mess Free

In 1904, the price of metal skyrocketed, forcing tea salesman Thomas Sullivan to change his methods. Instead of sending samples of tea leaves packaged in metal containers, Sullivan made small bags out of silk, filled them with leaves, and shipped these to his customers. He had created the first tea bag! Rather than dumping loose tea into a pot, now his customers simply dunked the bag into boiling water.

The first tea bags were a mess-free convenience that customers loved—and we still love them today!

Young Inventor Spotlight

Abbey Fleck

One Saturday, eight-year-old Abbey Fleck came up with a clever way to keep her family's kitchen mess free. That morning, her father had cooked bacon in the microwave. He ran out of paper towels and got bacon grease everywhere. To solve the problem, Abbey decided to invent a bacon-cooking dish. It had a square tray with T-shaped supports running across the top. When Abbey and her father loaded the supports with bacon strips and popped it into the microwave, fat fell off the bacon into the bottom tray. It was mess free!

Abbey and her father named their invention the Makin' Bacon Cooking Dish. Today, thousands have been sold to bacon-lovers worldwide.

Switched On!

Imagine a time before light bulbs existed. If you wanted to see in your home, you had to burn a candle or light a lantern. Sometimes, you would have been stuck in the dark! Twenty-two inventors tried and failed to invent the first practical electric light bulb. Luckily, in 1879, Thomas Edison succeeded.

The light bulbs of other inventors fizzed, flickered, and flopped. Some worked, but they were much too expensive to be useful for most people.

Long-lasting light

Edison built on the failures of others. He did hundreds of experiments with different types of **filaments**, or the threadlike wire on the inside of the bulb. When filaments are heated up with electricity, they create light. Edison knew he needed a filament that would be long-lasting and inexpensive. After testing 6,000 different materials, he discovered the key to producing the world's first long-lasting, affordable light bulb—a filament made from **carbonized** bamboo.

The carbonized bamboo filament in Edison's first light bulb could last over 1,200 hours.

Bamboo is a type of grass plant. Edison's idea to use bamboo in his light bulb came when he was examining threads off his bamboo fishing pole.

Fresh Food

Before freezers existed, people dried, canned, pickled, or salted their food to preserve it, or help it last longer. As a result, preserved foods often tasted different than fresh food. Clarence Birdseye can be thanked for showing the world how to preserve fresh food and not change the taste.

Many people today still preserve fruits and vegetables by drying (above), pickling, salting, or canning (below).

Frozen foods

While living in Labrador, Canada, in 1917, Birdseye noticed that **Inuit** people had a different way of preserving food. After fishing or hunting trips, they stored the food outdoors in the cold winter air. When the Inuit needed food later, they simply thawed and cooked the frozen meat. Frozen food tasted much fresher than food that had been perserved other ways. This inspired Birdseye to invent a freezing machine to fast-freeze foods.

By the end of the 1920s, Birdseye began selling packages of fast-frozen foods, supplying people everywhere with food that tasted as fresh as the day it was frozen.

Pop-Top

Today, opening a can of soda pop is simple—just pull the tab at the top. It wasn't always that convenient, though. The first pop cans came sealed much like today's cans of soup. To get to the refreshing drink inside, you had to use a can opener.

In old cans you needed to use a can opener to make a hole to get the soda out.

New design

Mechanical engineer Ermal Cleon Fraze changed all that in 1959. Fraze attended a picnic and forgot to bring a can opener to open his drink. He spent 30 frustrating minutes prying the can open on the bumper of his car. To avoid a repeat of this annoying experience, he invented a new can that had a pull-top lid. This new design no longer needed a can opener to open it.

Today, almost all canned drinks contain some form of Fraze's invention.

Young Inventor Spotlight Peh Yong

Drinking a cold can of pop isn't the only way to stay cool and refreshed, thanks to Peh Yong. At the age of six, the kindergarten student invented an umbrella with two purposes. In rainy weather, it prevented the user from getting wet. In sunny, hot weather, it brought cool relief by releasing **water vapor** on its user. Peh called her invention the Cooling Umbrella.

Super Suction

Sometimes, failure can be an inventor's best teacher. In 1901, engineer Hubert Cecil Booth watched another inventor demonstrate a dust-removing machine. The machine blew air into a carpet to push the dust out. More dust ended up around the room than was actually picked up!

Hubert Cecil Booth believed he could invent a better way to remove dirt from homes.

WINES

Squeaky Clean

Booth wondered what would happen if he reversed the direction of the air to suck the dust out of the carpet. He invented a gigantic suction machine called the "Puffing Billy." It was extremely large, and was powered by a gas engine to suck up the dust. Later, Booth produced an electric version of his vacuum cleaner, but it was just as large and awkward to use.

Fortunately, many innovations later, we now have smaller, more **portable** and powerful versions of Booth's vacuum cleaner to keep our houses dust-free.

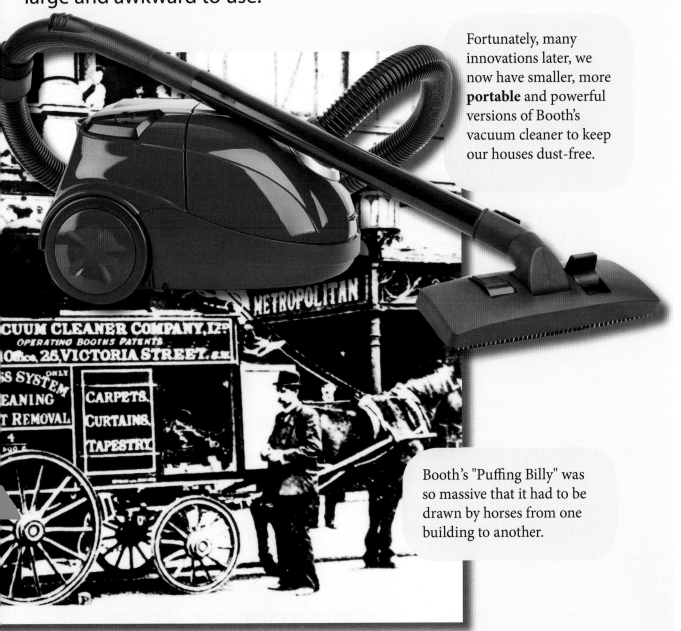

Booth's "Puffing Billy" was so massive that it had to be drawn by horses from one building to another.

Forever Blue

To make sure each batch of his pants matched, Levi Strauss dyed the cloth indigo blue.

Strauss added innovations to his original design, such as copper **rivets** to make pockets and seams stronger.

Did you know your comfy blue jeans were invented by Levi Strauss—to wear in dirty California mines! In 1849, during the California **Gold Rush**, Strauss tried selling miners **canvas** for tents or wagon covers. But the miners didn't need canvas for these things—they needed **durable** clothing to wear when they worked in the mines. So, Strauss hired someone to make pants out of his leftover canvas. When the pants sold in a flash, Strauss opened a small store in San Francisco. Eventually, he switched from canvas to denim, a softer, stronger material.

Young Inventor Spotlight

Chester Greenwood

Thanks to inventors like Chester Greenwood, clothing inventions can keep us healthy and safe, as well as fashionable. Imagine a cold, wintry day. The wind is howling and your ears are stinging. You need to cover them—or else you'll get frostbite! When 15-year-old Chester went ice skating in 1873, he wrapped a bulky, itchy scarf around his head. It wasn't a good way to keep his ears warm. To fix the problem, he invented earmuffs. His handy invention was so popular that eventually Chester opened the Ear Protector Factory to create millions of them!

The first earmuffs, worn here by Chester's great-grandson, were made of wire, cloth, and beaver fur.

FARMINGTON, ME. "The Ear Muff Capitol of the World"

The "GREENWOOD" Ear Protectors

Clearing a Path

In winter, snow can clog roads and stop traffic. It may pile up on your driveway—which means you'd have to do some heavy shoveling. If it's left to pile up, snow can completely stop people from getting around!

Snow Removal

Fortunately, Arthur Siccard invented a solution in 1925. When he was eighteen, Siccard spotted a farmer using a **threshing machine** in a field. As it moved, the long blades of the thresher spun, cutting stalks of grain and spitting them out the top. Siccard invented a snow-removing machine similar to the thresher. Its blades cut through the snow and spewed it out through a tube at the top. Siccard had invented the first snowblower! In 1925, he demonstrated his snowblower by driving it through the snow-plugged streets of Montreal. It cut through the snow and left a clear path behind!

Since Siccard's time, the snowblower has undergone many innovations. Today, they range from small portable home models for your driveway to large, truck-powered ones for streets.

Scaling Heights

Before 1857, elevators were raised and lowered by ropes. Sometimes the ropes broke, plunging the elevator to the bottom. For safety reasons, many people chose to climb the stairs instead. That changed, however, when Elisha Otis invented the safety elevator. He created a device, from heavy coiled springs, that would attach to the elevator and stop it from dropping.

Fear of Falling

To conquer people's fears, Otis demonstrated his invention at the 1853 New York Exposition. In front of a crowd, he mounted a platform. Once the platform was hanging high above the spectators, Otis's assistant cut the rope. Instead of crashing to the ground, the platform jerked briefly, then stopped. Otis's demonstration wowed the crowd. His safety elevator allowed builders to construct taller buildings and helped to bring in the age of skyscrapers.

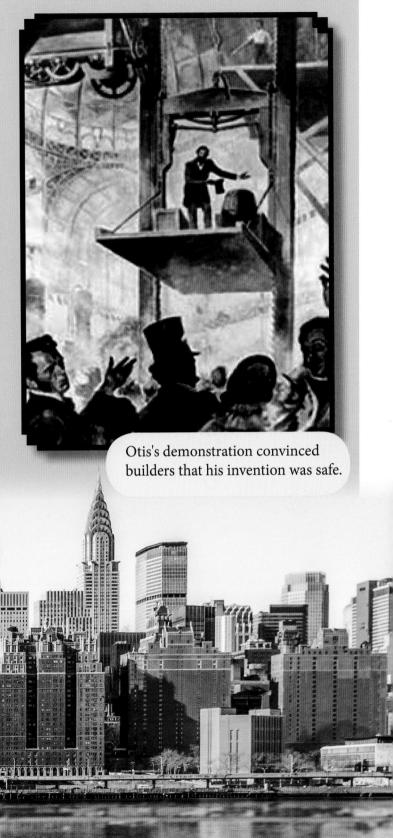

Otis's demonstration convinced builders that his invention was safe.

Thanks in part to Elisha Otis, big cities are now often filled with huge skyscrapers!

Small Inventions, Big Ideas

Safety Pin

In 1849, American mechanic Walter Hunt became **motivated** to invent a new product to sell in order to pay off a $15 debt. He started by twisting and bending a piece of wire, and within three hours created the first **prototype** for what we now know as a safety pin.

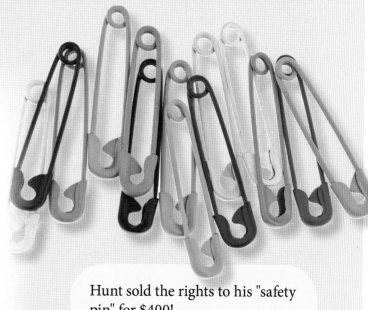

Hunt sold the rights to his "safety pin" for $400!

Toothpaste Tube

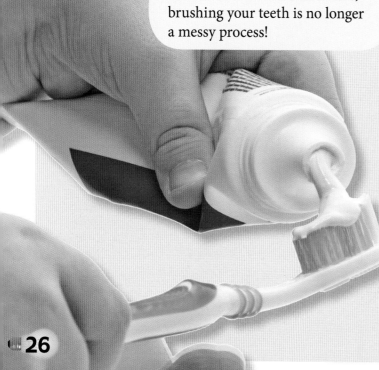

Thanks to Sheffield's invention, brushing your teeth is no longer a messy process!

Before 1892, toothpaste was sold in jars. People had to scoop out the sticky stuff and apply it to their toothbrushes. While watching artists at work, dental surgeon Washington Wentworth Sheffield noticed that their paints came in metal tubes. He decided to copy the design, but instead filled the tubes with toothpaste. Before long, all toothpaste was being sold that way.

Coat Hanger

In 1903, Albert J. Parkhouse was unable to find a hook to hang up his coat at work. Rather than throw his coat on the floor, he grabbed some wire, twisted it, and created a simple hanger within minutes. The idea caught on. Now coat hangers like Parkhouse's hang in closets everywhere.

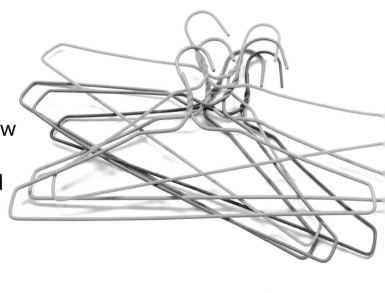

You, the Inventor

Inventors, innovators, and engineers follow a set of steps to solve problems and meet needs. These steps are called the Engineering Design Process. The steps in the process can be repeated as many times as needed.

Ask

What is a problem I want to solve or a need I want to meet?

Brainstorm

Write down all possible solutions.

Plan

Choose the best solution. Write a list of the steps you will follow and materials you will need. Sketch your design.

Create

Build a solution using your plan. Test to see how well it works.

Improve and Communicate

Review your results. Keep improving and testing your solution. Share your results with others.

Think Big!

Every invention or innovation in this book, whether large or small, started with a problem that needed to be solved. Now it's your turn. What problem will you solve? Is there something around you that is difficult to do? Does it take too long? Is it too complicated?

Think of a problem in your home, school, or community that you want to solve, or choose one of the suggestions below. Design an invention or innovation to solve it.

- Design a piece of furniture that creates more space in your room.
- Create a way to organize your messy closet.
- Think of a chore and find a way to make it easier!
- Could you make or store food in a new way?

Follow the steps in the Engineering Design Process to think big and solve your problem!

Learning More

Books:

Basher, Simon. *Basher Science: Technology: A byte-sized world!* Kingfisher, 2012.

Ceceri, Kathy. *Make: Paper Inventions: Machines that Move, Drawings that Light Up, and Wearables and Structures You Can Cut, Fold, and Roll.* Maker Media, Inc, 2015.

Challoner, Jack. *1001 Inventions That Changed the World.* Barron's Educational Series, 2009.

Wyatt, Valerie. *Inventions.* Kids Can Press, 2003.

Websites:

Visit this site for video clips and descriptions of new inventions and the inventors who made them:
www.abc.net.au/tv/newinventors/inc/categories/ InventionsByCat_DESIGN.htm

Learn more about inventors and inventions here:
http://inventors.about.com/

From the bread slicer to the cell phone, find out more about everyday inventions and the inventors who created them here:
www.enchantedlearning.com/inventors/us.shtml

This site will help you explore how to harness your own creativity:
http://inventivekids.com/

Visit this site for video clips of kids as they solve problems, invent solutions, and test products from hovercrafts to worm farms:
http://pbskids.org/dragonflytv/show/technologyinvention. html

Glossary

canvas A strong, rough cloth used for making tents and sails; also used as a surface for painting

carbonized To heat a material until it burns, creating the chemical element carbon

durable To be long-lasting, and able to withstand damage and wear

engineer A person with scientific training who designs and builds complicated products, machines, systems, or structures

filament The threadlike material in a light bulb that produces light when electricity passes through it

Gold Rush The rapid movement of people to gold fields; most commonly refers to the Gold Rush in California in 1848 and 1849

innovator A person who improves, adapts, or enhances an existing invention

Inuit A group of Native peoples from North America and Greenland

inventor A person who first comes up with a brand new idea, product, process, or device

microwaves Short electromagnetic waves created by an electric current; the waves used by microwave ovens in order to heat or cook food

motivated To be very enthusiastic about doing something

portable Something that is easily carried or moved around

prototype The first or early model of a product or process

rivets A short metal pin or bolt that holds two items together

thermostat A device that automatically controls temperatures

threshing machine A farm machine used for separating seeds or grain from the husks and straw

traits Qualities or characteristics that belong to a person

water vapor The gas phase of water

Index

About the Author

Larry Verstraete is an award-winning author of over 15 books for young people. Many of his books focus on scientific, historical, and true adventure themes. Larry lives and writes in Winnipeg, Canada.